Self-Care for Every Day

Self-Care
for Every
Day

Self-Care for Every Day

Reflections on Healthy,
Spiritual Living

Robert J. Wicks

For My Patients

Cover Design:
Scott Wannemuehler

Library of Congress Catalog Number
91-77633

ISBN 0-87029-238-2

©1991 Robert J. Wicks
Published by Abbey Press
St. Meinrad Archabbey
St. Meinrad, IN 47577

Contents

Part 1: Healthy Attitudes for Yourself   3

Daily Lessons to Improve Self-Esteem   5
Being "Out of Sorts"   7
Finding Silence in Activity   9
"Chronic Niceness" and Anger   11
The Value of Uniqueness   15
The Power of Negative Thinking   17
Emotional Difficulties and Hope   19
Joy and Laughter   21
Perfectionism   23
The Pain of Christian Leadership   25
Facing Suppressed Doubt   27

Part 2: Healthy Attitudes for Living   31

The Psychological Abortion of Adults   33
Security and Simplicity   35
The Elusive Route to Perspective   37
New Beginnings through Spiritual Reflection   39
Appreciating the "Now" in the Rush to the Future   41
Appreciating "Old" Gifts   43
Ways to Beat the Post-Holiday Blahs   45
Holiness and Pressure   47
He Has Everything...But Happiness   49
Worrying   53
Praying for Strength   55

Part 3: Healthy Relationships with Others — 57

Steps to Nondefensive Communication	59
Relationships	61
Giving and Receiving Love	63
The True Spirit of Helping	67
Forgiveness	71
Confrontation as a Positive Christian Force	73
Determining When Someone Needs Professional Help	77
Suggesting That Someone Needs Professional Help	79
Dealing with Others' Criticism and Anger	81

Part 4: Staying Healthy within the Family — 83

Accepting Ourselves, Accepting Our Parents	85
Problem Drinking and Unemployment	87
Spiritual Growth, Marital Discord	89
Spiritual Growth, Personal Vision	91
Sex Therapy	93

Acknowledgments

This book is based primarily on a series of articles I did for the *Catholic Star Herald* (Camden, New Jersey). I offer my deep appreciation to Jack Schibik, who encouraged me to write the column, and to Msgr. Charles Giglio, the executive editor, who continually encouraged me through his warmth and professionalism. In addition, I would like to note the support and enthusiastic spirit of Jacki Laird. She is truly a beautiful friend. Finally, and with the greatest sense of gratitude, I thank my wife, Michaele, for her editorial advice and personal generosity. Her deep faith in God and our Christian friendship have made the road we take with our beautiful daughter, Michaele, toward finding God each day a deeply rewarding journey.

Introduction

This shortened, revised printing of *Caring for Self—Caring for Others* (St. Louis: The Catholic Health Association of the United States, 1987) is designed to be a helpful "friend" for persons seeking greater psychological perspective and sound spirituality in a world often full of confusing and complex demands. The essays are brief and nontechnical. Each of them can be read in a few minutes and needs no special background or introduction.

These selections are my way of sharing a few ideas, feelings, and experience on some common problems and issues we face each day. They are not meant to be read all at the same time, nor are they meant to replace longer, deeper works. Rather, they are designed to help us quickly recognize that our problems are not unique and that responses are not totally beyond reach. These essays emphasize that with prayer, reflection, and some sound information, we will be able to see the end of the dark tunnel. A ray of hope is possible.

Doubt, stress, illness, depression, turmoil, burnout, confusion, failure—the list can seem endless and occasionally overwhelming for all of us, even those in the role of helper, care-giver, or minister. I hope the information that follows will not only provide initial help in dealing with these daily problems, but will also point to the need for trust in God and an openness to the Lord's presence when no solution that we find acceptable seems forthcoming.

Robert J. Wicks
Loyola College in Maryland
1991

Healthy Attitudes for Yourself

Daily Lessons to Improve Self-Esteem

All of us at times in life try to resolve one or more basic personal conflicts:
- Caring too much what other people think;
- Hearing praise in a whisper and negative comments as thunder;
- Being afraid to speak up and say what we really feel;
- Being unduly concerned about rejection.

Such issues usually point to a self-esteem problem. To deal with this, we must appreciate that they have both psychological and spiritual aspects. Psychologically, self-esteem issues originate early in life. The two primary sources are the way we were treated and the problems in self-esteem that our parental figures had.

No matter how much our parents—or the significant adults when we were young—liked us and tried to raise us correctly, many times they gave the impression that we were not enough as persons. If we were clumsy and spilled something, they might have said, "Watch what you're doing! You are so careless." They focused on us rather than on our clumsy behavior. Since this is a natural reaction, we are exposed all through life to this mini-attack on our person. And so we question our self-esteem.

When our parents lack security, we pick up some of their lack of confidence and carry on the "family tradition" with respect to how secure we are facing the world. Even when we are apparently more "successful" than our parents, underneath we may feel like charlatans.

Spiritually, low self-esteem comes from failing to trust completely that God loves us and that we are unique in God's eyes because we

Self-Care for Every Day

were created that way. Grace is a gift, and what we do—although important as a response to God's love—cannot earn us God's love, which is always there for us to enjoy.

What's the answer? How do we become self-confident and build up our self-esteem?

To begin, there is no complete answer. To some extent we will never feel completely confident—after all, this is not paradise and anxiety will exist until the parousia (the second coming of Christ). However, some simple, helpful steps can remove some of the unnecessary pain we feel in life:

- Imagery: Image yourself as a special person. Don't let the world tell you that you can become special by wearing certain clothes, having a particular job, enjoying many friends, or being well known. Instead, hold on with all your might and will to the reality of John's Gospel, which indicates that Jesus called us his friends, his brothers and sisters.
- Cognition: In your thinking, pick up negative thoughts and timidity and answer them; tell yourself you are thinking inappropriately. Replace each negative thought with a realistic, balancing, positive thought.
- Affect: When you feel low or insecure, look for the thought that is causing the feeling. Possibly you are personalizing something, exaggerating the negative, minimizing the positive, or making some type of cognitive distortion.
- Behavior: Act as if you are all right. This is not encouraging brashness or aggression. It is encouraging you to act, based on a trust in God that you are all right as a person. It is encouraging you to act in a way that corresponds to how most people probably view you—namely, that they find something special about you; they somehow see God in you.

Unconsciously, we are quite loyal to the negative. It is as if we learned a negative view of ourselves long ago and hesitate to give it up. Even when we get positive feedback, we feel less and believe this feeling as if it were common sense or reality. Such feelings are actually common nonsense. Maybe some things we do aren't good and need improvement, but we are always God's creation. If we trust in this, we will feel less insecure, be more able to do the will of God, and be more joyous and available to an anxious world that needs us.

Being "Out of Sorts"

There are times in the day, month, or year when, because of physiological reasons, we may feel swamped by negative feelings. We are more apt to become hypersensitive to negative memories and the way people treat us. We feel both sad and angry, and all the hurts, rejections, and disappointments in life seem to face us. Lack of sleep, daily stress, insufficient nutrition, inadequate exercise, and hormonal changes can all account for these periods. Certainly the period prior to menses is one of those times, especially for those women subject to particularly dramatic hormonal shifts.

During these times, our perception of the present and our recall of the past tend to be distorted. We see things through a negative filter, which then leads us to create patterns from our experiences that are not accurate. When this occurs, we seem caught. If we ignore what we are going through, we tend to become overwhelmed almost without our knowing it. This can lead to unexpected sarcasm or outbursts on our part. On the other hand, if we try to look at our feelings and thoughts, the situation doesn't seem much better. We wind up either condemning ourselves or indicting others. When these times pass, the temptation is just to give thanks and say, "Oh, I was just tired," or "It was my period; I'll just forget the whole thing." The only problem with this approach is that these times go by without any benefit to us. There is an alternative.

When hypersensitivity to others, sarcastic remarks, and "negative remembering" occur, we can take some steps to control and learn from the situation. They include recognition, silence, note-taking, and reflection.

The first step, *recognition,* is quite helpful because it alerts us to

Self-Care for Every Day

the fact that we are overly sensitive to how we are interpreting others' comments and actions. If we can pick up those times when we seem more vulnerable to life's normal rough spots and when we are more apt to look back at life's past hurts, we have made the first major step in dealing with physiologically induced valleys in our life.

The second step, *silence,* is helpful so we don't do something based on inaccurate perception. When I feel tired or for some reason "testy," I try to maintain as low a profile as possible and listen to my environment and see how I interpret it and the kinds of occasions from my past that I'm recalling.

The third step, based on what I have picked up during my "silent listening," is *note-taking* or writing in a journal about what I thought and felt during the day.

This leads to the fourth step, the key to the process: *reflection.* I don't do this reflection while I am still feeling low. I put the notes aside until I can think more accurately and positively. Then I look at them to determine what negative feelings are lurking underneath.

We need to evaluate unhealed memories and unfinished business so we can let go of them. As Henri Nouwen notes in his book *The Living Reminder,* if we continue to repress memories and feelings about how we were treated, they will persist in having a force in our lives, albeit an unconscious one.

Finding Silence in Activity

We are surrounded by so many demands: things to do, books to read, people to see, activities to take part in, prayers to say, good works to accomplish. The list is endless! We try almost anything to keep things under control. We make a list of things to do, which adds one more thing to hang over our heads—a list.

Our response is to feel we must do something or all will be lost. A better response, I think, is not to do something but to step back, be silent, and recognize our tendency to avoid silence by involving ourselves in compulsive activity. If we see some of our reasons for avoiding silence and can appreciate the lure of doing, doing, doing, then maybe we can transform our attitude about life and have the courage to set priorities better. James Whitehead wrote in an article called "An Asceticism of Time" that "Christian time management, as an asceticism, will always be understood as a response to grace, to the invitation to become less scattered and more aware of the Present already there.... Distress often arises not from doing bad nor failing to act, but, intriguingly, from doing too much good."

Brother David Steindl-Rast supports this point in his book *Gratefulness* when he says:

"We may have to learn that the useless deserves prime time. The superfluous comes first in the order of importance. The necessary will claim our attention anyway. To acknowledge this truth might mean a far more drastic transformation by divine glory than we were prepared to undergo. It might turn our set of values topsy-turvy. When Jesus says, 'Behold the lilies' (Mt 6:28), he is inviting each one of us to take beauty seriously in all its uselessness. What will this mean for our daily life?... The do-gooder is too busy. He has no

Self-Care for Every Day

time to bother with flowers...the busybody does not understand the language of...[the lilies'] silent eloquence. He rushes on. 'Sorry, I don't speak Lily.' His ears are buzzing with the din of his own projects, ideas, and good intentions."

Compulsive activity has the "advantage" of helping us to avoid silence, which can bring us to places we may not want to be. William Johnston notes in his book on mysticism that "when one's senses are no longer bombarded by all the junk to which we are ordinarily exposed, when the top layers of our psyche are swept clean and bare and empty—then the deeper layers of the psyche rise to the surface. The inner demons lift up their ugly faces." Parker Palmer puts this less dramatically but just as forcefully when he says: "I had come to the silence with a head full of religious ideas and beliefs. In the silence, they all fell away, structures without foundations. In the silence I was forced to confront the ambiguities of my own religious experience and I grew up angry about what I found there, about the discrepancies between my inherited faith and my own faithless life."

In addressing our overactivity, we must be willing to risk facing ourselves in silence and facing others who have expectations of us that include doing much and always being available. This isn't easy, but the alternatives—unbridled activity and undisciplined activism—lead only to an exhaustion of both mind and heart. When we are caught in a swirl of activity, it is a signal to us to seek God in it...to quiet down and let the depth of the quiet silently challenge us to form our days in a way that we don't run through them.

Let me quote a brief paragraph in a little work I did on the topic of availability. "Availability is a great gift; it is a gift to behold, a gift to cherish, a gift to share. Yet, as in any living gift, availability must be nurtured if it is to thrive and be a continual source of joy. The challenge is knowing how and when to do this; and the satisfaction is in knowing that if we continually try to be open to God, we will never lose it."

"Chronic Niceness" and Anger

Anger is a human emotion that is neither good nor bad; it just is. Like alcohol, it is not evil in itself and, just like alcohol, it can be abused. While most of us realize that it is wrong to vent our anger impulsively against others, we may not be aware of the problems at the other end of the spectrum, namely, avoiding anger at all costs to appear loving and accepting of everyone under all circumstances—or "chronic niceness."

Churchgoers and people in ministry and the social setting where they operate (church, religious community, Christian school) often support a style of behavior emphasizing control, suppression, denial of anger, and avoidance of conflict. As one might expect, such a philosophy can lead to personal devastation, apathy, or supposed religious causes that are based on legalism or extremism and unconsciously deliver hostility instead of the good news of the Gospel. Examples, unfortunately, are easy to uncover. Here are four obvious ones.

- The "nice" but insular and stagnant Christian church or school where officials are so fearful of having anger expressed in their midst that they discourage and deny conflict in any form.
- The accommodating priest or lay leader who gets along with everyone in the parish but develops an ulcer, hypertension and/or problems with alcoholism or obesity.
- The religious worker who does everything by the letter of the law and devotes much energy to keep from breaking it and to ensure that others don't venture out of its bounds.
- The Christian activists (e.g., for peace) who act with such a ven-

Self-Care for Every Day

geance that their message defeats the Christian one they claim to be delivering to others by witnessing the truth.

These examples of Christians not in touch with their anger, much less aware of their ability and need to use it constructively, can be traced to traditional misunderstandings that Christians have about anger.

Once we begin to see anger as being neither good nor bad and recognize it as a sign of personal vitality, we will be able to distinguish between *experiencing* anger on the one hand and expressing or dealing with it on the other. Christian assertiveness avoids both "swallowing" or denying anger and the opposite extreme of confusing assertiveness with aggression and trying to fight back by stomping on others first or in return.

Christian assertiveness is grounded in a belief that we as effective persons can and should recognize and understand what makes us angry. We should attempt to relate our anger to a specific issue, find the courage to own our anger, and ask "How did I make myself so angry?" rather than "How did he make me angry?" When we can ask this question honestly, we will learn to communicate our concerns in a way that does not unduly provoke defensiveness.

Christian assertiveness is also based on recognizing that we are angry at times with others because our needs or expectations are unrealistic. When they are realistic, however, Christian assertiveness calls for an openness that does not justify aggressiveness that drives others away nor glorifies passivity and prevents a free, real interchange. It deals with anger as it arises rather than when it blows up after being long buried in a sea of "niceness."

Owning our anger is essential not only to promote honest interpersonal relations but also to help us focus clearly on the validity of being angry at injustices and wrongs in society. Anger may be a sign of intense concern for others.

Anger can be a diagnostic tool to help us learn about ourselves, our defenses, our limits, and our beliefs. But we cannot do that diagnosing if we view anger as forbidding or if we bury it.

We should be sensitive each day to when and how we make ourselves angry. When we feel our "buttons" are pushed by something or someone, we need to ask "Why?" We can put the issue in specific, neutral terms and raise it to try to find a solution. And if our effort to communicate and deal with the problem doesn't work, we should

12

take care not to castigate ourselves or the person(s) at whom we are angry. Let us remember that patience is also a virtue.

Additional material on this is available in David Augsburger's book, *Anger & Assertiveness in Pastoral Care* (Fortress Press).

The Value of Uniqueness

We meet many people in our lives whom we respect and would like to emulate. They seem talented and self-assured and we think: "Why can't I be like them?" We may also see other persons doing things we perceive as important and we ask, "What am I doing with my life? What special contributions am I making?"

However natural this may be, we must recognize and address such fleeting negative references to ourselves. They contradict the fact that we are created in the image and likeness of God, that our talents are actually the footprints of God. The question we must ask ourselves is not how can we be like someone else but rather what is blocking us from the person we are destined to be in the eyes of God.

The Rabbi Zusya said a short time before his death, "In the world to come, I shall not be asked, 'Why were you not Moses?' Instead, I shall be asked, 'Why were you not Zusya?' " Instead of worrying about past time wasted and the "special" things you can accomplish in the future, look at yourself as you are now and ask what special gifts God has already given you.

E.E. Cummings said, "To be nobody but yourself in a world which is doing its best, night and day, to make you everybody else—means to fight the hardest battle which any human being can fight, and never stop fighting." The essence of this fight is to see your personality style for what it is, rejoice in its presence, and recognize the circumstances that make you "trip over" your style.

For instance, if you are a sensitive person, that's great! There are many callous people in this world. Thank the Lord for your presence. However, there is a cross to bear with this talent—as there is with every talent or personality style. Sensitive people sometimes become

15

Self-Care for Every Day

negatively oversensitive; they hear praise in a whisper and negative comments as thunder. The sensitive person should become aware when this happens and ask: "Why am I giving more credence to the negative than to the positive?"

Another personality style is that of the organized person. This style, too, is needed, especially in religious community living. (To function effectively, each local religious community needs three types of people: the evaluator who asks, "Did we do what we said we were going to do as a Christian community?"; the visionary who asks, "What should we be doing in the future?" and the organizer who asks, "Did we take out the garbage?" Yet the organized person can go astray, too, by focusing too much on the details and forgetting the overall picture. We call this the *gestalt*.

In God's eyes, we all have special personalities. Rather than try to become—or wish to become—like someone else, reflect each day on who we are called to be. One way is to ask: "What do people whom I respect like about me?" If they like your cheerful and supportive demeanor, then continue that behavior, all the while keeping a wary eye on that time when it becomes a problem. For example, you may cheer and support others but won't let yourself receive their support. Each day, then, can be a time to become more aware of self and better able to reach out to others. In doing this, you will be in better touch with the special part you play in creating the mosaic we call "the people of God."

The Power of Negative Thinking

People accuse many of us of being too negative. They say we never see the bright side and we have a bad attitude. We may agree, but sometimes we can't help feeling insecure; we are bothered when things go wrong. People may call this a bad self-image and suggest we raise our self-esteem.

Negative thinking is not unusual. Most of us have learned to give more credence to the negative than to the positive. We hear many positive things but allow one negative comment to discolor and disqualify the affirming feedback. We dwell on a single negative detail until it becomes so large that it blocks out reality. We need to recognize when we do this, then attempt to replace our negative self-talk with more realistic comments. Then we won't automatically accept the common nonsense we say about ourselves as if it were common sense.

To notice and correct negative thinking, it is helpful to recognize other patterns of faulty thinking:

Inappropriate generalizations and magnifications. We see a single undesirable occurrence or specific negative event as representing a pattern or symbolizing something more terrible than it really is. (For example, a person disagrees with us or is emotionally grumpy, and we believe that is evidence they don't like us or we are unlikable.)

Black-and-white thinking. If we don't achieve all our goals or don't reach our perfectionistic objective, we feel like a failure.

Negative mind reading. We anticipate negative results or assume people are thinking or acting in a negative way without having evidence or attempting to check it out.

Self-Care for Every Day

Uncritical acceptance of negative feelings. We accept our negative feelings as if they are based on something true, rather than try to uncover the negative—often faulty—thinking underlying them.

Faulty thinking, in general, is the source of many negative feelings about ourselves. Even if we have been so-called negative or hypersensitive persons all our life and have let any disruption or unpleasant happenings cause turmoil, we can change. The important initial step is to recognize negative thinking and answer it assertively rather than accept the unexamined assumption.

Part of the excitement of the Christian life is that we can believe God really accepts and loves us. If we doubt it, we need only look at the crucifix and see that fact there.

Trusting we are forgiven and loved should enable us to realize that we can be a gift to others so long as we don't accept the negative as truer than the positive. The rule of thumb is to learn from the negative. Don't exaggerate it or beat yourself with it. Self-love and self-examination should go hand in hand. When they do then, as children say today, we can be an "awesome" presence for good rather than tied up in unnecessary negative preoccupation, self-doubt, and self-criticism.

Emotional Difficulties and Hope

When suffering from fears, irrational thoughts, or some other kind of mental stress, a person experiences much tension and anxiety. At those times, it is natural to question faith and to wonder if there's something we're doing wrong.

Psychologically, if we get a thought that says, "I am not a good person, not trying hard enough," we should reject it totally as irrational and know that we are trying as hard as humanly possible. Spiritually, if we ever doubt whether we will continue to get better, we must remember Jesus' words in John's Gospel, "I will not leave you orphaned."

Even in the tough times when we are in turmoil and bound up with tension, we know that God is with us. In our prayer, we must picture a warm, loving God who trusts us, is satisfied with us, and wants us to relax. When we feel ourselves tightening up and our thoughts or fears running away with us, we should bring this image of God to mind. With the support of our families, a physician, if necessary, and God, we'll make it. We must have faith and remember Jesus' words, "Be not afraid."

Emotional problems, like mental stress, can be overwhelming and we may turn to the media for general advice. Although advice in a newspaper column or from a radio or TV show can be helpful, there is no substitute for personal professional help. We may need to discuss our problems with a physician, a counselor, or a priest.

We can present the problem to our priest, in writing if we choose, and ask him for a time to talk in confidence. Or we might choose to contact the priest under the anonymity that is the proper right of a penitent. For example, you could send an inquiry to him unsigned

Self-Care for Every Day

and ask for a written answer which you would pick up, say, next Saturday afternoon in the confessional.

Priests, as called leaders of the Christian community, are present to be consultants on issues that touch matters of faith. So all of us should avail ourselves of this help in times of mental or emotional stress.

Joy and Laughter

John Catoir, director of the Christophers, says in his book *Enjoy the Lord:* "After years of counseling priests, sisters, mothers, fathers, and teenagers, I came to realize how difficult it is for most people to be joyful. Life isn't easy and there are always problems to weigh us down. On the other hand, we were made for joy and there is in us a human faculty tuned to God's inner life of total joyfulness. It is the soul."

Being sensitive to injustices in the world is an important part of being Christian. Yet, if we are to do this in an ongoing way, we must have a theology of hope that trusts ultimately in the Lord. Although we are called to recognize, speak out against, and fight injustice, we must appreciate that amid all this thought and action, God is with us. This contemplative attitude of living enables us to be joyful and peaceful. It also helps us realize that, in facing the tough spots of life, we are not expected to solve all problems, but to face them with the joyful knowledge that God is with us when we are compassionate. People are not saints because they worry more or are better activists; they are saints because the truth they speak and the actions they take emanate from a joyful, gentle contact with God.

Psychologically, such joyfulness is tied very much to an accurate picture of ourselves, a picture formed when we take the time each day to pray and a picture formed through laughter. Norman Cousins, who wrote the book *Anatomy of an Illness* and was the only layperson to my knowledge ever to get an article published in the *New England Journal of Medicine,* said that laughter helped him when he battled a chronic disease. When he watched a comedy show on TV for about ten minutes, the belly laughter provided an anesthetic effect,

Self-Care for Every Day

allowing him to get two hours of pain-free sleep. From this he deduced that laughter is good medicine. The same can be said about laughter at ourselves—gently kidding ourselves when we become too inflated or serious. If laughter is good medicine, surely laughing at ourselves must be healing. As human beings, we have the gift of laughter—one of our distinguishing marks in the animal kingdom. Yet more often than not, we avoid using this gift to enjoy life's quirks and to tease ourselves into recognizing that while we need to face our responsibilities, we are made for joy.

A word on the importance of detachment. The late Urban Holmes III said in his book *Spirituality for Ministry,* "Detachment means our freedom from being victimized by our own emotions and those to whom we minister. The opposite of detachment is not compassion, it is seduction." Dr. Holmes cautions us not to try to meet the unrealistic expectations of others (that we can cure their problem in one hour, for instance) and our own unrealistic expectations (that we should be the savior instead of trying to do something good on behalf of the Savior). He implies that we should try to meet only God's expectations—to do what we can to reveal the Lord's healing presence by what we do, how we react, and most important, what attitude we display to others in need.

Perfectionism

Perfectionists often feel they're driving themselves crazy. As Christians, they may believe their approach is part of doing the best they can. But movement toward God does not require such intensity.

Wanting to be the best is a worthy and necessary goal. However, the way a person views a goal, rather than the goal itself, can be the source of difficulties. Instead of perfection being a goal that inspires people to be the best they can be, it may threaten them and make them feel not good enough.

In psychological jargon, many perfectionists are "shoulds" persons who experience a self-esteem problem. From a spiritual perspective, they may place themselves in front of a super-ego-oriented God who is saying to them that they are bad, sinful, and not pleasing.

One way they can deal with this is to take a few minutes for morning meditation to put themselves before an ego-oriented God, i.e., a God who is calling them in love to be all they can be and who knows failure is part of living a full Christian life. Then they won't see their failures as evidence that they are bad, but merely as human blocks to finding Christ within themselves and others. In this light, failures become opportunities to learn about oneself and appreciate dependence on God, not occasions for self-condemnation. When goals inspire persons, the result is a high degree of motivation; when goals only serve to threaten, the result is unnecessary depression and turmoil.

The Pain of Christian Leadership

A man was leading an adult group discussion on spirituality when two people who disagreed with several of his suggestions for reflection got up and walked out. The leader wondered later why he even bothered trying to help these people grapple with their spirituality, only to receive what he saw as abuse. He said that the incident took the joy out of his attempt to do the right thing. "It might be better if I just uttered pious platitudes and let them do and think what they want!" he reasoned.

I'm sure that anyone who deals directly with the public, especially in groups, has had this man's experience. The fact that a group is made up of "Christians" does not necessarily change the potential for such situations. It may even make them more likely because religion not only attracts the committed, the caring, and the charitable, but also is a magnet for the rigid and the self-righteous.

Another point worth noting is that people often don't realize how much of an impact they have when they are rude and close-minded. I remember giving a series of retreat talks when people wandered in and out and across the room where I was standing to address the group. I think they believed their actions just didn't matter because they had not been in a similar position themselves. The two people who walked out of the room when the group leader was talking probably didn't stop to think of his feelings. If they had, they wouldn't have been so rude.

A mistake we sometimes make is to personalize what people do or say to the extent that we make ourselves feel bad when we needn't do so. Once I was invited to give a brief talk to different groups that met each weekend. When I arrived, I saw people driving away or

Self-Care for Every Day

walking far from the building where the group was to meet. Because of my own crazy thinking, I said to myself, "I guess they don't care about me or don't like my material." Then it occurred to me that they not only didn't know I was the speaker, but they didn't know me. Their behavior was independent of mine, and I was making an erroneous connection between the two.

Another mistake we make is to use what cognitive psychologists call a "negative filter"—inordinately focusing on the negative and almost ignoring the positive. For example, when we get an evaluation of some sort, many of us tend to gloss over the positive comments, as if they are not important, and concentrate on the negative ones. In other words, we hear praise in a whisper and criticism as thunder. In my earlier example, two people walked out on the group leader, but many others enjoyed grappling with the issues.

That is life, particularly in leadership and service positions in the Church. We expect that when we turn the other cheek, people will be so edified that they will say, "My gosh, look at that humble person; he is so nice and right that I admire him and I'll apologize." What really happens is that when we turn the other cheek, psychologically, the rigid and the self-righteous take another swing at us.

The pain of Christian leadership isn't easy. While we do embrace in our commitment the peace of Christ, we must also at times carry his cross. Psychologically, we should try to lessen unnecessary pain by (1) recognizing that working directly with people is stressful so that we are not surprised by the pain; (2) appreciating the fact that people don't know how much they can hurt us through their rudeness and thoughtlessness; (3) not personalizing people's angry comments and actions; and (4) not using a negative filter so we hear the negative more than the positive.

Facing Suppressed Doubt

Belief and doubt have long been discussed as elements of faith in God. Yet, ironically, little has been said about one of the real causes of spiritual paralysis: suppressed doubt.

On the one hand, we have seen the results of trust in the Lord and almost hear Christ's words resound: "Your faith has saved you." In the Acts of the Apostles we can practically feel the deep trust of the people who believed in Christ's healing presence through Peter. "They all used to meet by common consent in the Portico of Solomon. No one dared to join them. But the people were loud in their praise and the numbers of men and women who came to believe in the Lord increased steadily. So many signs and wonders were worked among the people at the hands of the apostles that the sick were even taken out into the streets and laid on beds and sleeping mats in the hope that at least the shadow of Peter might fall across some of them as he went past" (5:12-16).

In contrast, the doubting Thomas refused to believe unless he, himself, experienced the presence of the risen Christ. We recall Jesus' statement: "Happy are those who have not seen and yet believed" (Jn 20:29).

There is yet another group of people who neither firmly believe nor loudly doubt. They are, I think, very large in number and are well represented among those who proclaim themselves as being "religious." They doubt but are so troubled by it that they have unconsciously or consciously pushed their uncertainty out of their awareness.

The problem is that even though they may not be conscious of it, their doubt still retains a force. Signs of this situation include a fail-

Self-Care for Every Day

ing to give first priority to daily prayer (If we believe in God, our relationship with God should be our most important activity during the day; all other prayerful activities would flow from this.); compartmentalizing God to a certain time of day or week without seeing the Spirit's presence in everything; relying on doing good rather than being good because they lack hope in God's action in the world; and anxiety over the evil in the world today (as if it is proof that God and God's power are but myths).

What can we do, given this prevalence of suppressed doubt and the potential harm that avoided and denied doubt can cause, even among those who proclaim a desire to be believers? I think we need to look at doubt as natural and part of the process of believing. In Thomas Merton's words: "You can't have faith without doubt. Give up the business of suppressing doubt."

The poet Rainer Maria Rilke wrote, "Be patient toward all that is unsolved in your heart and try to love the questions themselves like locked rooms and like books that are written in a foreign language. Do not now seek the answers which cannot be given you because you would not be able to live them. And the point is, to live everything. Live the questions now. Perhaps you will gradually, without noticing it, live along some distant day into the answer."

This is good advice. Doubt and question will always exist. Our choice is to look for God and ask for greater faith amid the doubt, rather than avoid doubt or ignore it in our lives. Prayer is a good place to begin because this is where we, each in our unique way, search for God and scream out for greater faith, greater love, and a deeper sense of courage to commit our lives to living the Gospel at each moment rather than thinking about it only several times a week.

Doubt also assures us that we are not in control. Its very presence calls us to be dependent upon God. In commenting on Matthew 14:22-32, William Hulme notes: "After a time the disciples believed they saw Jesus coming toward them walking on the water.... Impulsive by nature, Peter tried to find out. 'Lord, if it is you, bid me come to you on the water.' Jesus told him to come. Peter got out of the boat to do so. Then the Gospel writer says, but when he saw the wind, he was afraid and beginning to sink he cried out, 'Lord, save me'... (The implication is that had Peter kept his eyes on Jesus the story might have been different. But Peter deserves credit for knowing what to do when he was sinking—he cried out for help: 'Lord, save me.' Jesus immediately reached out his hand and caught him."

Living faith and lively doubt go hand in hand. It is in embracing both that we can live, not with the false expectation that our doubts will totally disappear but with the real hope that doubts, when we face them with prayer instead of panic, will lead to a more mature faith and a more creatively lived life.

Healthy Attitudes for Living

The Psychological Abortion of Adults

Einstein said: "He who can no longer pause to wonder and stand rapt in awe is as good as dead." This point has no greater validity than when applied to appreciating the loveliness of our own uniqueness as we respond to the Spirit that is calling us to be.

A woman who had a miscarriage in the final trimester of her pregnancy taught me the importance of the uniqueness of every human being. When I asked her how she felt about losing her baby, she said that she, naturally, was quite sad. "What tears me apart the most is that I shall never know who my child was...what he or she was like. Would he have been a hyperactive boy? Would she have been a pensive girl? I'll never know, and that is a special sadness for me."

We who do live, who have been born, and who have a personality that can be shared with others have a duty to let it evolve. If we abort our talents rather than let the Spirit grow within us, we mock existence and our singular place in it. Our absence significantly lessens the community (of saints).

Similarly, we must be aware of others in a way that is filled with awe and love. Just as we don't want to psychologically abort our own development, we don't want to close our eyes to the growth of Christ in others.

The issue of abortion is very serious and one that we emphasize when we think of the right to life. Yet, as the doctrine of the "seamless garment" suggests, we must look at the threat to life in every aspect of society. That is why we cannot concentrate on fighting the abortion of children while we simultaneously ignore the destruction of our own spirits. To emphasize justice for the unborn while being too hard on ourselves or uncharitable to others is illogical. The psy-

Self-Care for Every Day

chological abortion of adults needs to be faced as much as the abortion of the unborn.

We must see the challenge of charity as a priority. We must not "harden our hearts" and turn our backs on those who disagree with us, hurt us, are different from us, or those whom we fear. The beauty of the "Right to Life" movement is its call to all of us to love life right from the beginning. This beauty is tarnished when we become righteous or speak of religious principles with such venom that people see anger and hate instead of the love of God.

In practical terms, we need to turn to others in a respectful way:

- Listen to your children; don't just preach to them. They have a right to be heard.
- Stop categorizing people into "good" and "bad" categories but look for the presence of God in everyone, including (and maybe especially) those we view as manipulating, lazy, intrusive, too rigid, too liberal, too, too...well, too unlike what we want them to be!
- Don't return anger with anger but instead ask what anger is about.
- Don't look at others with the attitude of what they can do for you but see them as people to whom God gave a place on earth just the same as you.
- Don't look at others with all kinds of expectations as to how they should behave if they are to receive attention from you. (It is all right to smile and say "hello" to people who don't have the freedom to return the "hello." If they don't, that doesn't mean we were stupid to greet them.)
- Ask yourself each day—not with a sense of guilt but with a real interest in learning how to improve—how have I been open to the people I've met today? How was I open to friends, children, parents, colleagues, relatives, salespersons, everyone? If we ask this question enough, we will be psychologically and spiritually sensitive to the community (of God) around us. We may realize that the little "crumbs" of emotional nourishment we gave in a smile to a neighbor, a few moments of listening to our child or a co-worker, or a brief chat with a salesperson were enough "spiritual food" to feed a multitude.

Security and Simplicity

Sometimes we feel anxious almost from the moment we get up in the morning. Our thoughts go in forty different directions. We don't see solutions to any of our problems. We wish we could get some closure on the issues, conflicts, and questions we have. We feel there are so many demands on us. We experience a loss of joy. We become nostalgic for the times when things were simpler, when we could laugh more easily, when we felt the gentle presence of God more naturally, when a child's smile or the presence of a crucifix or icon made us feel that God was with us and we were with God.

How can we recapture this sense of inner peace in a world so full of turmoil? How can we appreciate what we have and stop the insatiable march toward wanting more and more? How can we replace tours of the mall that create a need for things we don't have with a walk down the street, a trip to the museum or library, or a bowl of popcorn to carry us through an old movie? Maybe with a return to simplicity, we can.

With simplicity, we see the void in our lives. We recognize the void as a sign that there is a God, that there is something greater than us, and we realize we can never fill the void without a spiritual relationship. With simplicity, we don't try to fill the void with food, money, possessions, drugs, alcohol, friends, power, fame, or personal accomplishments.

Life is certainly to be enjoyed, but it isn't designed to completely satisfy. Yet, we all fall into the error of expecting to be totally happy. Ironically, for those with some wealth, the problem can be even greater because we forget that the only security comes from depending on God. Rabbi Moshe Leib said, "How easy it is for a poor

Self-Care for Every Day

man to depend on God! And how hard it is for a rich man to depend on God. All his possessions call out to him: 'Depend on us!' "

To seek simplicity doesn't mean that we must give away everything and live a life of radical poverty like St. Francis. It does mean that we must raise our consciousness about how we are negatively influenced by the media, some well-meaning colleagues, acquaintances and friends, and themes and myths in contemporary society. I think Richard Foster is onto something when he says in his book *Celebration of Discipline:* "The modern hero is the poor boy who becomes rich rather than the Franciscan or Buddhist ideal of the rich boy who voluntarily becomes poor.... Covetousness we call ambition. Hoarding we call prudence. Greed we call industry."

Simplicity brings security. Simplicity encourages us to start each day putting our trust in God—not just with words but consciously, powerfully, and willfully in God. This means we say: "My security doesn't depend on what I own, who I know, how many people like me, and whether I succeed in doing all kinds of good things today (that preferably a lot of people notice). My feelings of peace are not destroyed by a loss of favor with others, a drop in the stock market, or a good grade. My security depends on one thing: an attention to the presence of God."

Simplicity also requires us to ask whether we need to buy something that will put us in greater debt. It requires us to ask whether we are doing more and more because we worry about what other people think rather than what God wants. It requires us to stop trying to control life and manage the upcoming weeks, months, and years so we can, instead, be open to enjoying today.

Simplicity takes the courage to let go of everything we have put so much faith in so we can enjoy all that is present to us. With a "spirituality of the now," simplicity calls on us to stop judging ourselves and others so we can have the energy to let others smile with us.

If you are like me, you already have too much. We may forget that each day we have the gift of the ability to walk or see or hear or breathe. Let's stop demanding and worrying so we can start enjoying life in a way that will also help others smile and see God.

The Elusive Route to Perspective

Several years ago, I was talking with an anxious millionaire. He was deeply concerned about his financial status. He claimed that even though a million dollars sounded like a lot of money, it wasn't really that much compared with what others had. Without thinking, I blurted out, "I wonder who your neighbors are." He interpreted this as a question and began listing the names of the chief executive officers of five Fortune 500 companies. I guess it's natural to think you're in need if you look out of his door.

In another session, I sat with a religious sister, a caring and committed person. She was concerned about those in her local community and spent sixty hours each week in her apostolate. She was worried that she was letting people down, that she was not there enough for them. I thought, "I wish you could see yourself in a positive light as I do. I wish you could appreciate how healing your presence is to people, especially when you are not worried whether you are doing enough."

Perspective is so elusive whether we are concerned about our material possessions, the service we do, or the view we have of ourselves. It is no wonder that so many people are depressed, anxious, or constantly striving for a goal they can never achieve. We search almost compulsively for the "right" accomplishment, the "final" investment, the "truly understanding" friend, the "perfect" job, or the "ultimate" educational program. Unfortunately, we are not conducting the search in the right place; thus, it is never ending and continually frustrating.

When this issue is raised with most of my patients, they ask, "Where should I look?" The implication is that I might actually

Self-Care for Every Day

know. I tell them, "It is not so much where you look as it is when and how you look."

You look when your mind first opens its eyes. While you are still in bed, turn your thoughts toward God—not in a pietistic way but in a manner that says, "During this day I shall remember you, Lord, your love of me, your love of others. These are not words I will take lightly or feel guilty over; these are words of the will that I shall take seriously and reflect on. If as you say, 'Those who do my will are my brothers and sisters,' I shall try to do your will and learn from those instances where I fail."

Continue this reflection later in the morning, sitting for ten to twenty minutes in quiet. Take the time to cement your commitment in prayer. During the day, turn back to your promises by remembering them for another fifteen or twenty seconds. As the day closes, wrap yourself in the warmth of God's acceptance and remember not only the day which may have tired you but also the friendship you have with God amid failures and efforts. The "when," then, is from dawn to nighttime in periodic doses. The "how" is in silence and gratitude.

New Beginnings through Spiritual Reflection

A funny thing happens to most of us every fall. Even if we are not in school, don't work in school, don't have children in school, or have not been in school for a long time, we seem to experience September as the beginning of a new year. Although January 1 gets the credit, the real new beginnings seem to belong to the first week in September.

It's as though our many years in school have imprinted the academic calendar on our psyche. Even nature can't convince us otherwise. After all, what happens in the fall? Leaves die, most of nature goes to sleep, and most of the green disappears. Nature tells us it is a new ending. However, Sister told us years ago it was a new beginning. Who are you going to believe? Right. Nature doesn't have a chance; we'll go with what Sister told us every time.

So if we are to make new resolutions and seek new ways to see God and let God be seen in us—our behaviors, attitudes, and visions—maybe fall is the time to do it. Maybe fall is the time to throw a party and get on our knees; to have renewed hope and a new journey in faith; to risk being Christian by seeing what exciting ways Christ is calling us to dump our domesticated faith and find the Spirit of Peace in a different way.

How do we do this? We've tried to do it in the past and it hasn't worked very well. Last January's resolutions fell apart before February. Well, maybe we shouldn't try to change. Instead, maybe this time—possibly for the first time—we should simply try to face reality and listen to God. When we do that, change will happen without our efforts; after all, doesn't holiness come to those who are open to grace? That's what I thought anyway.

Self-Care for Every Day

So how can we face reality and listen to God? I suggest the simple approach. It's so simple you may already be doing it so all you need to do is continue, the only change is that you do it with greater interest and—more important—with greater love. If you feel you already do this, check yourself to be sure you really do.

What I suggest is that five or six days a week you read a little from the Bible in the morning—maybe the day's readings from the lectionary—and stay quiet for fifteen minutes. Early in the afternoon reflect on what you've been thinking and feeling during the day. Do this in a way that helps you learn about yourself—not blame yourself or someone else for problems.

Then, at night, stay quiet for about five minutes. Take out an icon or a picture (of a field, a stream, a home...) that you can look at in love and appreciation for life and for God. (If you close your eyes during this quiet period, it can help; however, many people start thinking about a million things when they close their eyes after a full day.) Finally, read one spiritual book in the fall and winter. That's right—one. Your schedule is probably crowded and any more than one would be nice but impossible. Read one book as if it were the last and only book on earth. Read it in earnest, read it with love, and ask yourself: "What is God asking of me in this book?" If you feel guilty, it is not God speaking to you. Guilt is not going to help you focus on your blocks or help you learn; it's only going to make you feel bad. And isn't it silly to feel bad in your pursuit of God? Feeling bad will only make you give up.

Your pursuit should inspire you to ask questions. How can I make my life more simple? How can I share my love and stop trying to fill the void that only God can fill (through more possessions, trips, food, excitement...)? How can I learn to laugh more? How can I trust I am all right as a person so I can let down my defenses and my desire to control everyone and just be me, so people can be attracted to me because they see God in me and they see God's reflection in themselves?

Life really is simple. We make it complex and harder when we try to find justice and to be secure through our own efforts. On the other hand, we appreciate its simplicity when we seek God and love ourselves and those around us in a new way. Good luck on your new beginnings. And pray for me; I'm beginning again, too!

Appreciating the "Now" in the Rush to the Future

We seem to lament the passage of time. Most of us have said in a wistful voice at one time or another: "Time passes too quickly." Often we seem to be wishing we had more time, more space, more opportunity to enjoy the moments of life. And for those moments when something special did occur, we have photo album reminders.

However, with this attitude is a diametrically opposed one that shapes the way we face each day. It is a future-oriented vision that keeps us from exploring the "now" to see what it might have in store for us.

Parents often say, "I can't wait until she's in school, beyond adolescence, has graduated from college, has a good job (as evidenced by a never-ending string of promotions), is married, has children...." Most workers seek to somehow sweep away the week and exclaim in a relieved voice, "Thank goodness. It's Friday!" I think the real question we must face is "Why am I rushing through the 'now'?" Where are we going in such a hurry? Why is it that we are so willing to give up the opportunity to appreciate today—each day? If we are on a moving train going from Philadelphia to New York, we don't rush from the back of the train to the front so we can get to our destination more quickly; that would be ridiculous. Yet in life we seem to be constantly in motion, trying to get to the special times of the day, week, month, or year.

We look to the time when we can be this, do this, be secure, be happy. We act as if the present is devoid of reward and the future is a guaranteed time of plenty. As a result we miss so much, and by looking forward to things to such an extent, we don't know how to enjoy them when we get there. Instead we look ahead to further so-called

Self-Care for Every Day

rewards or feel frustrated that we can't enjoy what we've worked for and yearned for, for so long.

Each day as I drive to work and the same attitude tries to overtake me, I see a beautiful house that a man built for himself over a period of two years. He was so excited about the prospect of living there. I can understand why. It is a very nice house. But there is a problem. Just after he moved there, he died.

Each day is the only day we have. Each day, no matter how tedious our job, how many diapers our baby goes through, how busy our schedule, there are opportunities for us to *see...to respond...to appreciate.*

How we do so doesn't take a special talent or an inordinate amount of training. All it takes is persistence and attention to the ordinary and the incidental. Henri Nouwen told the story of the man who said, "My whole life I was complaining about interruptions to my work until I discovered my interruptions were my work."

One way I try to appreciate the "now" is by paying as much attention as I can to the person I'm with. (I don't always do so well, but the trying helps me to be more present than if I didn't try.) Another approach is to see people where they are—at this age, at this point in their life—as "gift." So if my teenager is a pain, I try to appreciate what she's going through, get involved in this time of her life, laugh at myself as I try to reason with her and usually fail, and try to appreciate our struggling relationship.

What's the alternative? Probably to run through life saying "Where did her growing-up years go?.... Boy, time flies, doesn't it?"

Appreciating "Old" Gifts

Special things sometimes get lost or are taken for granted and, in the process, they lose the unique quality they originally held for us. Some time ago Darrell Sifford, the columnist, interviewed me about this in the *Philadelphia Inquirer*. When I made my "confession" about how I keep things new and vital, my neighbors and friends teased me about it for months. I said that I often try to renew "psychological snapshots" in my life. I do things to remember the excitement and wonder of certain experiences surrounding people and things that are still part of my life today.

I remember the excitement I experienced the first time I walked into my house. I was a perennial apartment dweller and the house actually had a fireplace and a garbage disposal! (After buying the house, I discovered that the garbage disposal had no blade.) I mentioned in that interview that at times I stand across from my house and then walk into it, trying to image what it was like on the snowy day I first stepped into it.

If I don't do this, somehow I take the house for granted. I forget how lucky I am. That's easy to do because many acquaintances and friends have houses that are "better" or more unusual. When they visit, they may even criticize the house or go on and on about how I can improve it so it can be special. Also other houses in the neighborhood are as nice and it is easy to say "so what" about mine. So when I'm feeling that way, I try to recall the excitement I felt on my initial visit and the expression of awe on my mother's face when she saw the house for the first time.

The advertising media would have us believe that we require something more, something new. What we really need to do is dust

Self-Care for Every Day

off, rewrap, and open anew something we already have. Maybe that is the value of international travel and a benefit to those of us who were in the armed forces. We can more readily get in touch with how much we already have.

One of the national pastimes is to focus on what we don't have or have lost: "This friend and I no longer speak to each other." "I just missed investing in something good and look at how well the stock market has done." "I used to be able to do so much more but now I can't." "The church used to be...and now it's not."

The list of our lacks and losses is endless. The problem: we have lost perspective; we have lost the reality that all is gift. While we focus on the injustice in our lives, we fail to open our hearts and accept the love and many, many gifts that sit gathering dust, unappreciated, and unused right at our side...or in our families, places of work, congregations, and parishes.

Sometimes it takes a death, a loss, a crisis, or a traumatic awakening to blow the dust away. But it needn't take such an event. We can do it slowly each day because the dust of taking things and people for granted builds up on a daily basis. The question is: Will we take the time each morning, each day, each evening to look anew to basics and embrace all that is gift rather than give it away through neglect and a lack of appreciation?

Ways to Beat the Post-Holiday Blahs

Down periods are natural after a holiday like Christmas, but they can be transformed into a special time of the year if we are willing to do something about our attitude (thinking) and behavior.

Enjoy the quiet time. During the holidays we rush around shopping, going to parties, and preparing for Christmas. Then suddenly it's over. The tree is down and Christmas carols fall silent for another year. However, what we often fail to remember is that the Christmas season is not over for Christians. It has just begun. We can celebrate it in a thoughtful, relaxing way more in line with the real message of Christmas than the one that the media try to sell us. During the cold, quiet January and February evenings and weekends we can:

- Spend more time with the family. The holidays are such a rush that we rarely have time to converse or recreate at home with those we love.
- Read. Too often we get lost in the TV and move through the evening like a robot. You can still watch TV, but take out at least a half hour to read.
- Write a letter. Widespread use of the telephone has made letter writing a lost art. However, we can and do say things in letters that we can't say over the phone. If you feel you are not a letter writer, become one. Outline on paper the things you would say to someone in your presence, then write a paragraph for each point. (If you have no one to write to, write a letter to your local newspaper on something you feel strongly about.)
- Build a relationship with God. You have talked about prayer, read about prayer, and complained you don't have time to pray.

Self-Care for Every Day

Now you do. So pray. Take about fifteen to thirty minutes a day (preferably at the same time) to read a few verses of the Gospel or Epistles and just sit in silence and let them nurture you. Or read something spiritual (any book by Henri Nouwen, Thomas Merton, Anthony Bloom, or David Steindl-Rast should do if you don't have any particular book in mind) and reflect on what the author is trying to tell you about God.

Celebrate a different way. We are so used to celebrating the way society teaches us (big parties, for example), that we forget celebrations need not involve a lot of noise and liquor or drugs. The following are other ways to celebrate:

- *Take a Saturday morning family outing.* Combine a Saturday morning mass with eating out for breakfast.
- *Bundle up and go outdoors.* We are so mall-oriented that we fail to get the positive results of a short walk outside, a trip to a sports event, a walk in the town closest to us, a train ride to a nearby city, or a visit to friends and family missed during the holidays.
- *Invite friends over.* Although you may be "partied-out," a quiet evening with friends can be a relaxing community exercise that doesn't have to cost a lot of money or be very hectic. Lower your expectations and desire to impress others, get some cheese and summer sausage, and invite someone over for a couple of hours to chat, watch a TV special with you, or play Scrabble. It need not be a big deal.
- *Volunteer your services.* You may feel, "How is that going to help?" Or, "How is that celebrating?" When we reach out to someone else (and there are plenty of opportunities at the local parish, school, hospital, or community organization), it helps us to stop focusing negatively on ourselves. It is also a way of celebrating our gifts, good fortune, and faith in a way that leaves us with a sense of peace instead of a hangover.

The above are just some ideas. Try them or add your own, but the key is not to be inordinately pulled down by short periods of the blahs during the post-holiday time of the year.

Holiness and Pressure

Persons who are referred to as the "middle class" often report that they feel "fed up" with everything. These statements give flavor to this feeling: "I'm overtaxed, overworked, and overburdened. The harder I work, the less I seem to get ahead. When I go to church on Sunday and hear a sermon encouraging me to help the poor and be holy, I wonder how much more I can do and what else the Church or God expects of me. At the end of a hard work day, I often can't help feeling resentful."

Many, if not most middle-class people, have worked hard to get to their position and are holding onto it by a thread. If they hear the Church calling them to take on even more tasks in life—already filled to the brim—their anxiety is understandable.

However, I'm not sure the Church is calling us to do that today—to take on additional tasks in the name of Christ. Instead, I think the messages from sermons, writings, and parish groups that accurately reflect God's call is to "be holy, because I, the Lord your God, am holy" (Lv 19:1-4). The implications of this are important.

If we hear the Church's message as a guilt trip designed to make us work more, then that message has communicated the wrong thing. Rather, the Church—the institution, and in the broader sense of the term, the "people of God"—is supposed to help create a milieu in which holiness appears as something possible and desirable.

By holiness, I don't mean the pietistic notion of someone with hands folded, smiling serenely, looking like a poorly done plaster statue. When I speak of holiness, I mean an angle of vision—a perspective, a way of viewing, thinking, and acting in the world. In the words of James Fenhagen, the dean of General Theological Semi-

Self-Care for Every Day

nary in New York City, "Holiness...is a political word. A holy person is a person who sees the world if only momentarily through the eyes of Christ and is drawn to act in response to this vision."

In this troubled world where we are all under so much pressure, the call to holiness is not a call to add to our pressures. Rather, it is a call to view the world in a different way amid the pressures. Paradoxically, instead of adding things to our schedule, the call to be holy can actually transform it in such a way that we exprience more peace.

Persons I know who work under pressure and deal with many troubled people and difficult situations that would try the patience of a saint maintain their perspective with some simple steps.

1. They start their day with fifteen to twenty minutes (or more) of prayer and reflection. They read the daily readings from Scripture or some spiritual reading and sit quietly with it.

2. During the day, they reflect for a few minutes on how the day is going and their response to it. They don't blame themselves for the faults but learn from the experiences. Essentially, they pose the question, "What if I were to die now? Would my thoughts, actions, and feelings be appropriate in the light of the Gospel?"

3. They read Scripture at night (or some time during the day) with a sense of surprise. Again, in the words of James Fenhagen, "The question we ask is simple: What is it about this passage of the Bible that suggests a new way of viewing the world or forcing us to see differently?"

These steps are not the be-all or end-all. They are designed to help us transform our day so that it all becomes holy. Prayer and reflection are not a call to do more but to be more. If we can see our whole day—work, play, at home, in church, at the supermarket—as being God's day, then we will not separate our lives into two parts: our part and God's part. We will look for God and bring God everywhere—in family interactions in the morning, chance meetings with neighbors, interaction with co-workers, community worship on Sunday. Remember, it is possible to do many so-called good things and still not live in the spirit of holiness, just as it is possible to live a life the Lord molds yet appears ordinary to all who look on. The difference is in our outlook. Do we mold it or does God mold it?

He Has Everything... But Happiness

All of us probably know the type of man who is a real "go-getter." He's gotten far in business. Bright and energetic, warm, trustworthy, and dependable, he may be about fifty years old, a senior executive with a major company and financially well off. Yet he doesn't appear to be happy; everything seems to annoy him.

Many males in this age group—whether executives or not—become frustrated, feel exploited, and lose their appreciation for life. Contributing factors may include age, decreased opportunities, and many psychological, physiological, and social changes they are experiencing.

It is not unusual, then, to hear men—or women—in this age group say:

- "They [children, friends, co-workers] don't appreciate me."
- "I feel like I'm hitting my head against the wall. The harder I work, the less money I have" (or "the less I accomplish").
- "I'm getting tired of doing the same things; life just isn't much fun anymore."

Along with the attitude problem, there may be increased use of alcohol and a reduced ability to enjoy creative leisure time. A man may pull back, even from his spouse, because he feels misunderstood. His wife, for her part, may feel she is in a no-win situation. If she tries to point out his inappropriate thinking or hypersensitivity, he gets angry and says she's not on his side. On the other hand, if she tries to ignore his outbursts and remains quiet, he accuses her of not caring about him. The situation seems hopeless.

Self-Care for Every Day

When I work with a man like this, I agree with him that he does indeed deserve more out of life. Then we proceed to examine what he can do to become more alive, more receptive of all life has to offer. My goal is to accept the right of the person to experience joy while I help him to understand and change those behaviors that are interfering with an appreciation of life.

Most men in this category, however, will still remain defensive and declare it is not their fault that their attitude is poor. I agree with them. It isn't totally their problem. However, I also emphasize that they project blame onto someone else. They give away their power as well. The question for facing any problem is: What can I do to affect my destiny?

For instance, a man at this age may feel he has done so much for his children that they owe him. He translates this debt into an unrealistic expectation that they will meet his (often abruptly changeable) needs and respond completely to his unspoken requests. Instead, he can adjust his expectations, seeing what he has done for his children in the past more in the sense of *mitzvah* (giving without expecting anything in return). By making his needs and requests more clear, he will get more of his expectations met and be less frustrated, thus enjoying his children's presence more and making them more interested in being with him.

If his occupation or finances frustrate him, he needs help to step back and try to be open actively to the joys that are already in his life. To some extent, we all buy the world's version of success. The forties and fifties are ideal times to pull back from being duped, to stop comparing ourselves with those we see have more, and to begin to appreciate life less in terms of quantity and more in terms of quality. Too often we confuse quality of life with quantity of life. We spend waking moments chasing some image of success the media sells instead of God.

The essential goal is to help a man in this position realize that it is natural to experience some sense of loss and frustration at his age. At the same time, these limits can lead to greater creativity and depth which will uncover his achieving new ways of appreciating life. Instead of living under the tyranny of this stage, drawing into himself or ventilating without doing anything, he can find satisfaction developing a new way of relating to self, the world, and God. Assertiveness, more openness to positive comments, greater flexibility, and development of new skills are all waiting for the person who can

50

let go of old expectations of self and others.

Finally, if a person is not willing to let go, then patience from those close to him and/or several sessions of growth counseling would possibly be the best approach. While they're trying to have an impact on him, however, close friends or relatives must keep in mind that no one can force growth on anyone.

Worrying

Even when everything seems to be going well in life, many of us can't resist searching for something to worry about or blowing things out of proportion. We seem to be preoccupied constantly with the negative. We may recognize that this style is unproductive and want to do something about it. But that can be difficult when we've been this way all our lives.

Worrying is not just a serious drain on our energy level; it is a waste of energy. In addition, worriers turn people off. Who wants to be near a person whose implicit philosophy of life is negative? In the extreme, worriers are like "silver linings" always looking for the clouds.

However, this style can be altered even if people have been this way for most of their lives. Every personality style has a positive and a negative side. There is a fine line dividing the two. For worriers, often the other side of the line is being a concerned person.

Concerned people are great. They see the issues, are sensitive to others, and can appreciate some of the factors in their own lives that need attention. The difference between the worrier and the concerned person is attitude.

The worrier's style is based on anxiety and the desire to control; the concerned person's style is based on reality and the ability to trust. The worrier becomes *preoccupied* and ruminates over problems, whereas the concerned person becomes *occupied* with a problem and plans or acts according to an assessment of it.

Henri Nouwen, in his book on the spiritual life *Making All Things New,* addresses this problem directly when he says: "To be preoccupied means to fill our time and place long before we are there.

Self-Care for Every Day

This is worrying in the more specific sense of the word. It is a mind filled with 'ifs.' We say to ourselves, 'What if I get the flu? What if I lose my job? What if my child is not home on time? What if there is not enough food tomorrow? What if a war starts? What if the world comes to an end? What if...?' All of these 'ifs' fill our minds with anxious thoughts and make us wonder constantly what to do and what to say in case something should happen in the future. Much, if not most, of our suffering is connected with these preoccupations."

What can we do then if we are a worrier? How can we transform our preoccupations? The approach we need is as much tied to our spirituality as it is to our psychology. We must try to consciously increase our trust in the Lord as much as we try to let go psychologically of those things we cannot control. These are steps we can take each day:

- Say a morning prayer for trust in the Lord, for the belief that the Lord will stand with us no matter what we face. Also, recollect this desire during the middle of the day and as we go to sleep.
- When a worry bothers us, occupy, not preoccupy ourselves with it; break down the problem and plan an approach rather than ruminate on its sad or negative qualities and focus on our helplessness.
- Limit ourselves to how long we will spend planning a strategy so we don't let it fill our entire day.
- Finally, avoid the "savior complex" by recognizing our limits and the Lord's limitless power. In a sense, we should stop taking ourselves seriously and begin taking the Lord more seriously in prayer.

If we do this, we can address real concerns directly and not let unnecessary pain (neurotic worrying) make the situation worse. Then, for example, when a friend or relative is sick or dying, we can face the issue by praying, appreciating the gift of our own health, planning how to be present to the person, and seeking to find with the person God's gentle presence amid the pain of the situation.

Praying for Strength

In times of trial, some people pray for God's intervention with a rigid set of expectations as to what God should do. In most cases they want God to reestablish the status quo. For example, if they have lost health, money, or a job, they want God to intervene and return it to them. Still others ask God for help in a situation, but in their hearts they really don't want help in the form of assistance; they want to be rescued. They want God to go into a difficult situation while they wait in the background unscathed. It's as if they are saying to God, "You walk into the battle and get crucified, but I'll be right behind you so I can be there in time for the resurrection."

The alternative to these approaches shouldn't be to go it alone. That would be dangerous; we would be distancing ourselves from God, failing to develop a sound spirituality/theology of hope, and building up the illusion that we actually can handle life's crises beneficially by ourselves. The fact is we need God. When we don't call upon God, we run the risk of falling into despair, confusion, skepticism, or a self-reliance that can easily grow into self-worship.

Crises are mysteries in which we can find God and grow, but they are also times when we can despair and move away from God. In prayer, we need to ask God for strength, to stand with us, and to help us uncover God's love amid the pain. When faced with pain, we should have low expectations (based on what we want) but high hopes (based on what we and God together can achieve in love).

Too often what prevents us from finding God in life's pain is focusing on its cause. We ask, "Why is this happening to me? What did I do to deserve this?" We seem to be blaming God for our troubles. If we follow this to its logical conclusion, we are left with two negative

Self-Care for Every Day

possibilities: either God is heartless or we are very guilty and deserving of punishment. Therefore, if we or someone we love gets cancer, either God doesn't love us or we have done something wrong to merit this pain. Of course, this is far from the truth.

The world in its freedom has been given the gifts of water and air, and in its freedom it has polluted them. From such sources people are bound to get sick. When this happens, praying for strength and healing is appropriate and needed. The answer may come in the form of an obvious miracle—physical healing. But we must also be open to other answers from God. During the mystery of pain, some people look only for the miracle they are seeking. If it doesn't come, they feel abandoned. Others in pain are open to help in any form it comes; they open their ears to the Spirit and they hear God. Their faith is strengthened.

We must try to join the latter group and seek God every day, even in our pain and confusion. As Rabbi Harold Kushner points out in *When Bad Things Happen to Good People,* it is not the source of pain but the result of it that is important. The outcome for some is bitterness, for others, growth. How we seek God is the key. And the fidelity with which we see Christ as the door is the Way.

Healthy Relationships with Others

Steps to Nondefensive Communication

Defensiveness is such a waste of energy. It limits the joy of interpersonal relations, destroys initiative and creativity, lowers a person's or group's morale, and distorts communication.

Both predisposing and precipitating factors cause deficiencies. Predisposing conditions are low self-esteem and high sensitivity. The lower our self-esteem, the more we are vulnerable to attacks or perceived attacks from others. Hypersensitivity makes the situation more acute; a person's radar is up constantly seeking negative comments or circumstances in the environment to relate to the self to make it feel bad. Persons like this have a sensitivity to negativity analogous to fly paper—anything possibly negative they can personalize, they do.

Precipitating factors that lead to defensiveness are quite varied. In some cases, it is natural to be defensive. If someone is personally attacking us rather than criticizing some aspect of our behavior, to react—possibly without reflecting on it first—is understandable.

Other causes include defensiveness from the person we are interacting with, fear of rejection, exaggeration of criticism, inappropriate expectations without reason (expecting people to attack us or to react negatively), feeling someone is questioning our abilities, a suggestion offered at the wrong time—in front of others, for example, or in an emotional/threatening way.

Defensiveness is fairly easy to observe from the outside. People, however, may not be as quick to observe it in their own behavior: "I am not angry and defensive; I always shout when I feel you are judging me!" Some of the more obvious defensive reactions are rigidity, attack, withdrawal, and camouflage. When someone is unable to be

Self-Care for Every Day

open, keeps repeating a stand, and doesn't seem to have understanding or empathy for another's position, rigidity is evident. Attack can be in the form of an overt insult or the "long war" of passive-aggressiveness. Withdrawal can appear as "niceness"; a person may appear to be listening and comprehending but, in reality, is gripped in anxiety, responding in what seems to be a positive way to avoid further openness and intimacy. Camouflage can involve focusing on a detail or topic, diverting attention from the problem at hand, or hiding behind a principle or rule so the bigger issue is kept at bay.

The following are guidelines to help diffuse defensiveness and to develop nondefensive communication techniques:

- Increase self-esteem by having a more accurate, positive picture of self. If we assume we are all right as people, we will be less apt to be defensive even if others are.
- Deal with issues, not people. Stay away from name calling. If people do it to you, bring it to their attention and divert them back to the issues at hand.
- Try not to predict failure in advance. The more you are open to the possibilities of an interaction and the more you lower your defenses, the greater the chance for a nondefensive encounter.
- Be specific, clear, and adult in your communication. Don't move all over the board or be vague or patronizing. Be honest and to the point in bridging your understanding with the other. Don't prejudge and precondemn, but deal with the issues of misunderstandings in a way that makes handling the problem an exercise in learning.

If these techniques fail, a cooling-off period may be in order. Take time away from discussing and come back later when tempers cool and space for sharing is present again.

Relationships

Openness and a healthy, clear appreciation of your own personality are probably two of the most essential building blocks in the formation and growth of relationships. Relationships are beneficial when they are open and free. The more conditioned we make them, the less healthy and mature they are.

The limits we place on others and the limits we feel we must respond to from others are often unnecessary and destructive. We are tempted to fool ourselves into believing that certain conditions are merely understandable expectations. Yet in our hearts we can recognize the fallacy of this by the negative feelings and tensions those conditions engender. Any relationship that can't be trusted is not worth having.

During his Genesee experience, Henri Nouwen came to this realization in his appreciation of how easy it is to limit and distort even the most beautiful interpersonal experience open to us, the one we call "love." He said, "It is important for me to realize how limited, imperfect, and weak my understanding of love has been.... My idea of love proves to be exclusive: 'You only love me truly if you love others less'; possessive: 'If you really love me, I want you to pay special attention to me'; and manipulative: 'When you love me, you will do extra things for me.' Well, this idea of love easily leads to vanity: 'You must see something very special in me'; to jealousy: 'Why are you now suddenly so interested in someone else and not in me?' and to anger: 'I am going to let you know that you have let me down and rejected me.' "

Opening up a place in our heart for others so we might be available to them, and in turn to be gracious enough to appreciate the

Self-Care for Every Day

warmth of their gifts of self, is a difficult mystery of living. Because as people we tend to be so needy, there are many nuances of openness that can be violated without our even knowing it. In the words of Thomas Hora, "To be interested is to love and revere; to be inquisitive, however, is to intrude, trespass, violate."

To have healthy relationships with others, we must be clear about our relationship with self. The relationship with self determines how we deal with the world and how we view ourselves. View of self and the world at large is unique to each person. No matter how much someone likes or hates us, knows or is unfamiliar with us, no one will ever view us or the world quite the same way we do. The reason is that we are unique. In psychological terms, we each have a singular feature called "the personality."

So to understand our relationship with others, we must first appreciate how we relate to ourselves. If we are relaxed with ourselves, we will be at ease with others. If we feel insecure in terms of our own self-esteem, we will constantly be comparing ourselves with others. Relationship with self goes hand in hand with a relationship with others. As Pope John XXIII noted, "Whoever has a heart full of love always has something to give."

Giving and Receiving Love

Probably the biggest problem I encounter in my therapy practice is people's inability to give and receive love. Many who come to me are unable to experience love when it is present or give it without a lot of strings attached.

Many of us have had difficult experiences in childhood or are undergoing them now. Feeling others' love and sharing ourselves are quite difficult then. The only answer is to open our eyes to the love that is in the world, our world, and to give with a spirit of *mitzvah* (to give without expecting anything in return).

As I write this, I am thinking of a person I meet about once a week. When we meet, I smile and ask, "How are you doing?" She usually complains that no one appreciates her and she doesn't get a chance to be what she is able to be. Generally she has a depressed look. I wonder if she presents such a negative picture to each person she meets and if that is, perhaps, part of the reason people avoid her or treat her in a negative way. I wonder, too—actually doubt—whether she is a bit happier having experienced my smile and interest in her. My heart tells me "I hope so" but my head says, "My smile probably rolled off her back, whereas anything that she probably could interpret as negative stuck like glue." However, any time I'm tempted to give up on her, joining others who probably have, I remember a story Mother Teresa told.

> We have a place in Australia. When we went around in that place we found an old man in a most terrible condition. I went in there and tried to talk to him and then I said to him, "Kindly allow me to clean your place and clean your bed and so on." He answered, "I'm all right!" I

Self-Care for Every Day

said to him, "You will be more all right if I clean your place." In the end he allowed me to do it and when I was in his room I noticed that he had a lamp, a very beautiful lamp but covered with dirt and dust. I said to him, "Do you not light the lamp?" And he said, "For whom? Nobody comes here. I never see anybody. Nobody comes to me. I don't need to light the lamp." Then I asked him, "If the sisters come to you, will you light the lamp for them?" He answered, "Yes, I'd do it!" So the sisters started going to him in the evening and he used to light the lamp. Afterwards (he lived more than two years), he sent word to me through the sisters and said, "Tell my friend, the light she lit in my life is still burning!"

As lovers, we must persevere. We must have low expectations and high hopes. We must also be open to love wherever and whenever we experience it. William Johnston, S.J., says in his beautiful and profound book, *Christian Mysticism Today,* "...the great challenge of the Christian life is to receive love, to open our hearts to the one who knocks, to accept him into the very depths of our being...authentic human love is God's love made incarnate. So accept the love which comes your way. If you think that nobody loves you, this is probably because you are subconsciously warding off love. You are just not taking it in. Accept it with gratitude and you will experience joy."

Loneliness and feeling a lack of love is a serious and common problem in the United States. Mother Teresa sees it as a deeper poverty than the kind in Ethiopia and Calcutta. "To the hungry there, you give them bread and their eyes light up in love and gratitude; to people here where bread is plentiful, the hunger for love is the problem we face."

What is the answer? I don't know the answer, but I do have a not very original response. It follows the one Jesus gave and the two people I've quoted. Accept love wherever and whenever it is given, and give it with a sense of *mitzvah.* And strive to share love from the innermost circle outward.

In other words, we must love the Lord by loving his presence within us—we must love and respect ourselves. Then we must love our family and those we meet each day, even if they are grouches. We must love those in every part of our city, state, and wherever, rather than concentrate on whether they are getting more from life than we are. Naturally, this is a tall order, but we have the rest of our lives to strive to fulfill it. Finally, we must seek to embrace the smiles, good words, and friendship others give us, not desperately and by trying to hold onto and smother the person who shares with us, but gently and respectfully. In William Johnston's words once again, "Accepting love, we [need to] return it not only to God but also to people—to everyone we meet without exception."

The True Spirit of Helping

Being a sensitive helper isn't easy. A woman who often helped others said that she thought most people appreciated her assistance. She also noted, however, that sometimes others took advantage of her, were sarcastic, or vented their anger on her. Because she was quite sensitive, she would feel terrible, would wonder if she was too good to people, and then would withdraw for a while. Eventually, she would start the process all over again. Others would tell her to "toughen her skin" but she didn't feel right being callous or rude to people.

Sensitive people like this woman are beautiful. Caring is necessary—especially in a world intent on personal survival and narcissism. How can we preserve the sensitive, caring person so that her love can continue and she experiences no undue pain?

Neil Richardson once noted. "Jesus taught that God was not only more demanding than people cared to think, but also more generous than they dared to hope." In helping others, we need to respond to both the Lord's demand and the Lord's generosity. In responding to the call to reach out to others in need, we have to face the reality that hurting people hurt others—including those who wish to help them.

A few common examples:
- The adolescent in the turmoil of physical and emotional changes who is disrespectful to parents and teachers because he is so confused inside.
- The single parent who vents her anger on the director of religious education because of the diocesan guidelines she must follow if her child is to be confirmed.
- The frustrated co-workers in need of a break from a tough year

Self-Care for Every Day

who are starting to get on each other's nerves.

The list is endless.

When we reach out to such hurting people, they will often respond in a negative fashion. Sometimes we are surprised by this; we feel that if we assure others and help them, they will do the same for us. We turn the other cheek and expect that they will be overwhelmed by our goodness. Instead, psychologically, they hit us right in the face.

When this happens, we should not take it to heart. Often their reaction—or the extent of it—is not directed at us. On the other hand, we shouldn't ignore it because letting them be angry and hostile without bringing it to their attention doesn't help either. Instead, we might say: "You seem angry. Are you angry at me, or someone or something else?"

If we are troubled that people are not appreciating us or are taking us for granted, this is a sign that we are either not setting limits for them or our expectations are unrealistic. People will often ask for unrealistic attention or help if we give them the signal that we won't say "no." Also, sometimes we forget that we help not because we want others to appreciate us as a wonderful person but because we want to share Christ with them, to be holy. As Kenneth Leech notes in his book *True Prayer,* "Holiness manifests the character, the nature of God.... Holiness never points to itself but always beyond itself to God. The saint is essentially someone who communicates and radiates the character of God, his love, his joy, his peace.... And the world needs saints, Simone Weil wrote, just as a plague-stricken city needs doctors."

To gain perspective and continue helping in a world filled with stress and bent on destruction because it believes it can fight hate with aggression, we need love, both to give and to receive. We must be willing to receive it from others in the way they smile, struggle, and try to live in a tough world.

When you see someone who doesn't appreciate your efforts or who has a temper, don't take it to heart. Remember that somewhere in their broken heart is God. Maybe you are not the one chosen to reach them, and that is all right. Don't fall into the danger of disliking yourself or the other person if you don't feel like your helping is making a difference. Sometimes only God knows when and how we make a difference.

Most important, when we feel we are getting nowhere and no one

68

seems to appreciate our efforts, we need to move closer and closer to God in prayer. As Teresa of Avila says: "He never tires of giving...let us never tire of receiving." If you feel just as terrible in prayer as in other parts of your life, don't worry—just stay there feeling terrible...and your patience will be rewarded. Instead of feeling unloved, unappreciated, and unaccepted for what you do and who you are, you will soon feel a peace amid the turmoil. And it is in the field of peace that real joy—the joy of the Spirit—grows best.

Forgiveness

Forgiveness is important for both spiritual and psychological reasons. It is the cornerstone of our relationship with God. It is also the basis for our ability to learn about ourselves and experience Christ in others.

Since prayer is an experience of relationship with God, as long as people have a hard time believing they are forgiven, they have a hard time praying. The two—believing God forgives them and having a relationship with the Lord in prayer—go hand in hand.

Sometimes people say their head believes they are forgiven but their heart doesn't. Maybe it is more accurate to say that intellectually they grasp the possibility of forgiveness but they come directly up against their underlying belief that this just isn't so. They need to confront the belief that they are unworthy persons by admitting it and then realizing that despite this fact, God loves them. Or in the words of Pierre-Marie Delfieux: "Even should your heart condemn you, God is greater than your heart." Judas and Peter graphically portray this in the New Testament. Both let Jesus down. While Judas could not believe in God's forgiveness and despaired, Peter could conceive of it and became a cornerstone of the Church.

Psychologically, forgiveness is of great value, too. It enables us to be open to our mistakes and failings without anxiety. When we fall, we can learn. When we appreciate both our sinfulness and God's great love, we can approach one another, not as people who are lost and not as the self-righteous who are saved by our own efforts, but as sinners who seek to learn how we might better receive God's grace.

By psychologically holding on to the mystery of God's great love, we open ourselves to the action of the Spirit in our lives. St. John, in

Self-Care for Every Day

his Gospel, uses the word "paraclete" for the Spirit, a word suggesting among other things, the action to "animate," "exhort," and "comfort." By recognizing God's love in our minds and holding it there by determined will, we can ask in prayer for help to overcome our lack of trust in this love.

C.S. Lewis once noted: "...we want to know not how we should pray if we were perfect but how we should pray being as we now are." In our prayer we must be honest. We must admit our doubt if this is what we feel, but we need to hold on tightly to our faith. A prayer like that, based on truth and humility, is one of the best we can make.

Finally, we can reflect on the words of Robert Faricy, S.J., in his small book entitled *Contemplating Jesus.* I had the pleasure of working with him on this book and in it he says, "Jesus loves me. He does not love me because I am great; he loves me because I am not. He didn't come to save the just. He loves me in spite of my sinfulness; he loves me partly because of my weakness, my frailty. It is a characteristic in me that he can respond to with compassion. My weakness and sinfulness provide the 'opening' to his salvific love."

Confrontation as a Positive Christian Force

Confrontation and Christianity seem to make such terrible companions. Often confrontation is absent when it should not be or, when it is used, it is indirect or manifested inappropriately as the "holy interpersonal hammer" of God. These situations are unfortunate. Not only are people hurt when ill-planned confrontations crush them. But they are also deprived if they are not confronted when a confrontation is necessary for their continued Christian growth.

In a book for those in active ministry, Ralph Underwood notes: "To move beyond borders of empathy to consider confrontation in pastoral ministry may appear to be like entering an alien land. The difference is striking. In empathic listening, the pastor's own viewpoint is held in check to assure accurate and caring understanding of the other person. In confrontation, a perspective other than the parishioner's own is introduced. Usually empathy helps people expand and develop what they themselves have introduced. While one may hope for readiness, confrontation ventures to help persons face facts or issues they may not want to consider…. Respect is a moral connection that discloses how empathy and certain ways of being confrontive require each other.

"Respectful, considerate confrontation goes hand in hand with empathy. This is not the kind of confrontational attitude where one says, 'It's my job to hit people between the eyes with reality, and what they do with it is their business.' Rather, respectful confrontation communicates in essence, 'Having gained some understanding of you, I now trust you to deal openly with some things you have not considered.' That is, for all their differences, there is no fundamental

Self-Care for Every Day

contradiction when ministers who are empathic are also confrontational, so long as there is respect. Such an understanding of pastoral ministry is critical if pastors are to be faithful to Christian tradition, including its ethical dimensions.... By listening, pastors adapt themselves to others. When this posture is not balanced by challenging persons to consider others' perspective, it runs the risk of encouraging people to idolize their own self-understanding.... Confrontation, then, invites persons to extend and enrich their participation in community."

Although written for those in pastoral ministry, the above comment can be made to every one of us. However, knowing that confrontation is an essential aspect of communication and knowing when and how to do it are two different things. Although the issue of confrontation is delicate and complex, some basic points can be made.

First of all, respect is essential. Without it, confrontation will result in a mere victimizing of others.

Second, we must—as part of this respect—be willing to confront others as an equal. By that, I mean there must be an openness to change our views, confront our own feelings, thoughts, and way of viewing the world, as we help others confront theirs. Not to be open to this simultaneous confrontation is to be closed, defensive, and lacking the willingness to grow that we are asking of those whom we are confronting.

Third, we should have developed a trusting relationship with those we confront so that they can believe we have listened to them, understood them, and are empathic to where they stand.

Fourth, in confrontation, we should be specific and unpretentious in our approach. On being specific, Professor Underwood writes: "Concreteness anchors understanding, intensifies it, and prepares a person for genuine change in identifiable ways. General insights foster self-satisfaction and produce little change."

If we deal with a specific issue, we can often reach a general conclusion and application. However, if we are too vague, we are often left with a general insight that never seems to apply in reality. As for unpretentiousness, confrontation should be part of the natural interaction between two people (sinners) walking together to God rather than a professional helpful dictum from on high. Here our attitude toward ourselves is just as important as our respect for others.

Fifth, we should present observations that are confrontational in a tentative fashion. This way, the person confronted can participate in confronting the situation or perspective. Such mutuality helps to convince the person of the reality of our respect.

Sixth, in confronting, we need to own our contribution to the issue being dealt with; not to do so is to deny that relationships are dynamic and involve all participants. Such self-disclosure breaks down the barrier between the confronter and the person being confronted. The situation is more mutually open, satisfying, and growthful.

Confrontation isn't easy. We often are anxious about conflict. Sometimes we use it as a method of revenge rather than help. Other times people misunderstand and think ill of us because of our candor. And still other times, we are not clear and respectful and thus mess up the encounter. However, even given all this, confrontation is necessary if Christian community is to remain alive and growthful. The goal in Christian confrontation is to encourage people to be all they can be without embarrassing them as to who they are and what they are doing in life. Since we are all human, we will occasionally miss the mark; but if we have respect for others and are willing to be open ourselves, confrontation can open up new opportunities to receive God's grace.

Determining When Someone Needs Professional Help

One of the best ways to determine whether someone needs professional help is to keep these questions in mind when you listen to the person relate his or her difficulties:

- How exaggerated or severe is the behavior problem?
- Is the problem or are the symptoms unusual or bizarre in nature?
- Is the person baffled about the cause or solution to the problem?
- How much is the problem interfering with the person's overall daily activity?
- Does the behavior seem to be getting worse?
- What has the person already tried in an effort to deal with the problem?

The severity of the problem is one key in determining whether a person should seek professional assistance. Feeling a bit down, anxious, or confused is not cause for alarm in itself. Only when the situation becomes extreme should a person seek outside help.

A good example is the grief reaction. If someone close dies, the survivor is naturally depressed. This could last for some time, ranging from weeks to possibly months—even years. The person, particularly a spouse of thirty or more years, may have periods of the blues for the rest of his or her life. This is not undue cause for concern.

However, if the person is severely depressed month after month and begins to develop physical ailments and seems unable to adjust at all, the situation may be abnormal. The key is the severity and duration of the symptoms and the observable signs. If the reaction is

Self-Care for Every Day

out of proportion to the cause in terms of magnitude or persistence, it is usually wise to seek outside help.

Outside help may initially be a physician who can temporarily prescribe a psychotropic drug (one designed to affect behavior or mood) or a member of the clergy who can provide support. If the problem persists, referral to a psychotherapist may be necessary.

Some situations that may indicate the need for a professional mental health evaluation include: persistent, severe depression; overwhelming anxiety; frequent loss of self-control (for example, frequent verbal or physical anger with inability to prevent its expression); incapacitating guilt; extreme hesitancy in dealing with daily problems; continual preoccupation with personal health; great irrational fears (phobias); persistent marital difficulties; spiraling family problems; inability to adjust to change; excessive drinking, gambling, or use of prescribed or illegal drugs; chronic sleeping or eating problems; inability to develop good interpersonal relationships; difficulty in holding a job; serious school problems; extreme dependency reflected in an inordinate fear of independent, adultlike behavior; great difficulty in relaxing; little ability to concentrate; compelling desire to please others—and the fear of not being able to do so.

In addition, if a person's symptoms are unusual (hearing voices not actually present, having irrational fears that people are plotting against him/her), if problems baffle the person and it gets worse to the point of interfering with daily activities, or nothing seems to work in dealing with the problem, then professional help may become necessary.

Suggesting That Someone Needs Professional Help

Telling people they may need professional help for their emotional or mental health can be an ordeal because of the stigma attached to seeking such help. Actually, therapy can be viewed in desirable terms. Some people feel psychotherapy is chic, particularly if the therapist has the right address, high fees, and a well-known reputation. For a time (and still in some circles) being in analysis with professionals was the "in" thing. On the positive side, many people are in therapy because they are talented and involved. If they weren't so committed and gifted, they would not have become so overwhelmed.

Most of my patients now are really "stars" who seek help to gain perspective because of the stress and pressure that come from being on the cutting edge of life.

On the other end of the spectrum, therapy is viewed as a stigma. Some families see therapy as proof that people can't work out their own problems; consequently, they are weak. They don't realize that persons in therapy may be there to further actualize capabilities and strengths that are temporarily stymied.

Families may also object to therapy because they see it as proof of their own failures. Instead of encouraging a troubled or upset son or daughter to get outside support, they fight it. They believe that if the child goes to a therapist, they have failed as parents.

Even the "liberal" segment of society may harbor mixed feelings about therapy. They readily recommend it for others, but it's like pulling teeth for them to admit they need it too.

Remember these points when recommending outside help to others:

Self-Care for Every Day

- Be clear and direct about why you are suggesting they consider consulting an expert about their problems.
- Be clear in your mind about what you want to say before you mention the topic. Have your own feelings about therapy clear in your mind, too, and be aware beforehand of the response you may get. This will reduce the chance that you will seem self-conscious or that the other person will feel uncomfortable because of your uneasiness.
- Raise the topic in a private place. This is a serious and personal issue. It should be given the privacy and attention it deserves. If a person responds by joking, don't jump in and fool around. Some people laugh when they're nervous. You don't want to convey the feeling that emotional distress is funny or unusual.
- If a person expresses repugnance at going to a "shrink," describe the role of a clinical social worker, psychiatrist, or psychologist in terms of a specialist in interpersonal relations and mental health. People don't usually hesitate to go to a medical specialist or a lawyer, so why should they balk at another type of specialist who can possibly facilitate their handling an issue? One definition of therapy is that it is an intensified version of the normal process of growth.

You can encourage a number of books that could be helpful. If you follow these guidelines and leave ample room for a person to react and ask questions, you can usually broach the topic of therapy in a beneficial way with a minimum amount of discomfort for the helper and the person being helped.

Dealing with Others' Criticism and Anger

A principal of our elementary school shared the following dilemma with me, hoping to find an answer to the pressures she found herself under. "When I was a teacher, everyone was afraid of the principal. I have strived to change this attitude by being more open to criticism from parents as well as the teachers. However, I'm starting to feel burdened by the anger being dumped on me. Did I create a monster by being so willing to hear negative comments?"

Leaders who are closed to criticism are apt to have a distorted view of their organization—be it a school, church, business, or another type of institution or interpersonal team. Ironically, people like this often don't even know they are closing the door to possible negative comments. They may forestall criticism by minimizing it, reacting sharply, viewing it as disloyalty, or being pollyannish when faced with difficulties. What results is a distance between the leader and those under her or him, along with a lack of group vitality and generally poor morale.

Yet, when one does open the door interpersonally, anger and negativity, as well as all the positive elements that come with openness, can and usually do result. The answer when this happens is not to pull back, however, but to deal with the negativity in a different way.

First, try not to personalize and absorb the anger or complaint. People who offer criticism may have a good point about what is wrong; however, if you take it personally and feel they are blaming you, you will be defensive. Separate the complaint from the complainer and the issue being addressed from yourself so you can give it a good hearing.

Second, try to get people to be specific in the comments and sug-

Self-Care for Every Day

gestions they've offered for improving the situation.

Third, if possible, get the person who is complaining involved in the solution. For instance, if a person complains about someone, ask if he or she has approached the other. If not, encourage that. This requires their facing the issue instead of dumping it on you.

When others try to put me in the middle by telling me things with the proviso that I not tell someone else, I usually say, "I'm sure you wouldn't want to put me in the middle, so if you are going to tell me something, you'll have to stand behind it." Sometimes people are quick to complain and suggest actions but don't see the implications of their proposals. For instance, in an elementary school, a teacher might request a different grade to teach. You could ask the teacher what to do with the teacher already in that position or how to deal with others who might also have their eyes on it.

Fourth, no matter how healthy and effective we are in dealing with anger, the residue can build up. Leaders, because of their constant visibility, are bound to incur the anger of others, sometimes rightly, sometimes due to miscommunication and/or another's undue sensitivity or expectations. When such a build-up occurs (1) I tease and laugh at myself to diffuse the strain I've put myself under by trying to meet the expectations of everyone; (2) I maintain a low profile for a bit and surround myself with sympathetic, supportive people. I don't seek out empathic problem-solvers at this point but people who will say, "Oh, you poor sock, how could so-and-so treat you so horribly, especially since you're such an angel and you haven't made a mistake since 1949"; and (3) I eventually get people to problem-solve with me to break down the complaints and analyze the anger so I can develop strategies to deal with them honestly and effectively.

Failures, small and large, whether we are directly responsible for them or not, are part of life. The more we worry about them and what people think, the more we will be pulled down.

When people complain and we can see that we have failed, I think we can take a page from the life of Christ, who had to deal with what the world would have viewed as failures in his mission. As John Navone, S.J., aptly notes: "The endurance of failure in any of its many forms is a requisite for salvation; hence, authentic Christian discipleship is an education for failure." Anger and negative criticism directed at us aren't of themselves very important, but doing everything in our power to learn from them and live through them with perspective and belief in God's love for us are important.

Staying Healthy within the Family

Accepting Ourselves, Accepting Our Parents

Adults can still feel five years old when they deal with their parents. They may be trying to please their parents or proving to them that they really are adults and are truly "somebody."

Unfortunately, this problem is all too common. When we are young, the significant people in our lives are usually our parents, and these parents, because they lack sufficient psychological resources, treat their children in a way not based on acceptance and love. Instead, their love is conditional and they give the message: "You are not good unless you do what we want." Often another underlying message complicates the first: "You will never be able to do what we want."

Since these messages are subconscious ones—most parents are not consciously malicious—and often nonverbal (a gesture or facial expression), they are communicated first when the child is small and can't speak and are imprinted on the child's subconscious.

They remain as the child grows into adulthood, unconsciously controlling the person unless he or she brings them out into the open and deals with them assertively and courageously.

Too often we think we are dealing effectively with these messages when we try to prove to our parents that we really are all right. However, under all our efforts there remains a loyalty to the original parental message: You are not all right—no matter what you do. Consequently, even if we accomplish a lot and people applaud us, we still feel like charlatans and we still look to our parents and other rejecting figures in our environment to say we are all right. We hold on to the original image of ourselves that our parents gave us, even though we know intellectually that we are better than that image, bet-

Self-Care for Every Day

ter than the way we feel about ourselves and believe our parents feel about us.

As a result, we feel a gnawing hunger for acceptance. We vacillate between anger and sadness toward the parents we have because we feel cheated that we don't have the parents we deserve. At times, we may absent ourselves from our parents or argue with them. At other times, we try to do everything for them so they won't have anything against us and will finally accept us. The whole business is confusing and exhausting. The question we seem to be asking is: "Why can't I accept myself and accept that my parents aren't going to change?"

This question leads to frustration and the feeling that it has no answer. But it really is a good question and deserves to be answered assertively every day. In spite of our feelings (actually the unconscious negative schema we received in childhood), we should dare to accept ourselves and proceed in the world as if we were all right. In reality, we are! Like a pilot at high altitudes, we have to be guided by instruments and not our eyes. Pilots who fly at high altitudes by their eyes and not their instruments can end up flying upside down because they believe they see the horizon correctly. The instruments that must guide us are the acceptance that comes from our friends and the unconditional acceptance that comes from God.

Another kind of acceptance is necessary here—our acceptance of our parents. I did not say resignation; I said acceptance. This is an active process of looking at the givens, understanding them, and living with them. By having realistic expectations, we no longer look at our parents in a way that sets us up to be disappointed. It is hard—almost impossible—to accept the reality that our parents are not (never have been and probably never will completely be in the future, even if they mellow) what we would like them to be. But it is this acceptance of reality, this acceptance of our cross in life that will set us free to live rather than chase illusions.

The power is in our hands to accept—not in our parents' hands to reform. The sooner we grasp this message and live it without looking back or panicking, the sooner life will become a reality we live instead of an existence we complain about in sorrow. And with acceptance, we will be able to feel the mother and father love that is all around us in our friends and acquaintances and even in the glimmers that may appear from our parents.

Problem Drinking and Unemployment

A common problem that affects many couples today is drinking due to unemployment. A man who once had steady work in a trade has recently been able to get only part-time work at a minimum wage. Since the income and benefits are inadequate, he has looked for other jobs. The only response he gets from prospective employers is "Fill out an application; we'll look it over and call you." They never do. To make matters worse, he has a drinking problem; consequently, when he doesn't get a job, he turns to alcohol to "solve" his problem. His wife has a hard time with this. When she tells him he needs help, he denies it and the problem is compounded.

Unemployment and problem drinking are common unhealthy companions. When people have dedicated many years to an industry and the rug is pulled out from under them, it is a blow to their self-esteem and to the financial stability of the family. Unfortunately, more and more companies today are replacing long-time steady employees with part-time workers at a minimum wage. The negative impact on persons in their fifties and sixties is devastating. Consequently, turning to an "old friend" (alcohol) that was part of celebrations in better times is not unusual. Of course, this only compounds the problem.

During periods of unemployment, drinking encourages denial and brings on nostalgia. Neither helps. It is important to have a clear head when seeking employment. It becomes even more difficult with heavy drinking. Alcohol provides temporary comfort and a guarantee of long-term problems, not only for the person unemployed but also for the spouse. The serious danger is that a spouse may give up and the situation becomes a slow martyrdom.

Self-Care for Every Day

There are things that such couples can do. The direct approach with problem drinkers rarely works when they are in the denial stage, but for the spouse to sit back and let the situation continue to destroy her or him is not the answer. I suggest that such spouses call Al-Anon, where there is usually round-the-clock service. The Al-Anon representative can discuss the problem over the phone and put spouses in touch with someone like themselves who can guide them in dealing with the situation and thus preserve their sanity.

For the unemployed partner, the county department of vocational rehabilitation can help. It usually offers an employment service which includes vocational/growth counseling. He or she probably has talents from previous jobs to use in other areas. The spouse should encourage and support the unemployed partner wherever possible and seek the help and support needed.

Spiritual Growth, Marital Discord

People who enter spiritual direction usually find it rewarding. Speaking to someone about one's prayer life and relationship with God is joyful. However, this new situation can sometimes cause friction at home. A spouse may tease the person about becoming a "Holy Roller" or say the person pays too much attention to God and less attention to him or her. The person in spiritual direction may not know how to handle the problem.

Change, any type of change be it good or bad, causes some degree of stress. Someone may react to a spouse's participation in spiritual direction simply because of the change in the spouse's habits or because the spouse's energy seems to be siphoned off from other areas. This is a natural result of getting involved in something new.

A husband or wife may also feel threatened by the relationship with the spiritual director and the possibility that a disciplined prayer life might alter the spouse's outlook. This, too, is not unusual and has a parallel for people who enter counseling or psychotherapy. In these situations, spouses often feel somewhat competitive with the counselor and they, initially, may worry about the impact the treatment will have on the marital relationship. In most cases, when they see the positive results, their concern lessens. Eventually, good-natured kidding about the whole process may replace concern.

Informing a spouse about spiritual direction may help to ease stress or anxiety Knowing that a spiritual director helps someone on a regular basis (once a month, four times a year, etc.) with a focus on his or her relationship with God, one realizes that the director is a knowledgeable person one feels comfortable with, not a friend we turn to in order to fill an interpersonal void in our life.

Self-Care for Every Day

Persons in processes like spiritual direction can also prevent undue stress if they look at their own comments and behavior. If spiritual direction is having a good impact, they will model healthy behavior. They won't be trying to proselytize people which would merely reflect their own insecurity and need to be affirmed that they are, indeed, on the right road. As Christians, we should attract people to Christ and encourage them to be all they can be by letting them see our peace, enthusiasm, and sense of purpose, not by embarrassing them about where they are at a particular point in their lives.

If anything, spiritual direction should actually enrich a marriage in the long run. Being drawn more and more to God, the person will likewise be drawn to the community of Christ on earth where the spouse is at the heart. But spending more and more time in church and less and less time with spouse and family is likely to indicate not that the person's prayer life is becoming deeper but that he or she is withdrawing from life inappropriately. A tendency like this needs discussion with the spiritual director.

Spiritual Growth, Personal Vision

If there is one word that summarizes the message we give our children as they grow up, it is *accomplish!* The person entering young adulthood often translates that word, with the help of a consumer-oriented society, into two words: *consume* and *compete!*

Those words become the theme for many adults in marriage and the workplace. The big job, the big house, the big salary are the music; winning is essential, being number one is success, and being known and powerful is the only goal worth seeking in life.

Fortunately, the Church, the Bible, and humanists in society help modify these messages. We begin to see the importance of thinking of our neighbors in concrete ways (for example, sharing money, clothing, and food) and viewing them in a broader context (the "global village" where we are citizens, with all peoples of the world, of the Kingdom of God). Yet even with these changes in outlook, we still focus primarily on ourselves, our jobs, our homes, our vacations, and our future security, like having a million dollars in our retirement fund. Spiritual direction and development can, perhaps, alter that outlook. This is where the conflict begins.

Spiritual growth can radically affect one's personal vision and thus unsettle the previous equilibrium of the family outlook. Let's take the case of Bill Johnson (a fictitious name). He is a corporate executive with a wife and two children. Up to now, he has been competitive and security-minded. His wife is content with this; her satisfaction comes from feeling secure in his accomplishments and high income. The big house, the portfolio, and the children tucked away in private schools are all part of the picture.

The focus of the family to this point has been where they will

Self-Care for Every Day

move next, what promotion Bill will attain, how early and on what salary he will retire. Then Bill begins to step back and examine his life, maybe without the aid of a director, per se. He decides to take time each morning for daily prayer in solitude with God, a short afternoon reflection, and some scriptural/theological reading for a half hour in the evening. Although this sounds "harmless"—after all, how could a little religion hurt?—and even though he has no dramatic conversion or "born again" experience, he begins to question his life and his goals. He still wants to be a corporate executive, live comfortably, and get the best education possible for his children, but his vision has changed.

Instead of envisioning a bigger house and retirement fund, he may want a smaller house. Instead of focusing on who to entertain to increase his chances for career advancement, he may want to interact with those he believes will challenge him to be all he can be *in the eyes of Christ*. The result? The spouse (and the gender can be reversed in this scenario) is confused, in conflict, and not sure whether they share the same vision anymore.

At this point, communication, patience with each other, and the guidance of an experienced director or a counselor familiar with this natural outcome of spiritual development would help. The only danger lies in panicking or disregarding the feelings and beliefs of either party. Before a revisioning in marriage, there is always confusion and with growth there is also some pain. The alternatives—a marriage formed by a philosophy that doesn't have God as its center or one that is not alive—although they may seem better because they provide temporary peace—are surely not desirable in the long run.

Sex Therapy

Intimacy is the cornerstone of a good marriage. Through conversation, spending time together silently, sharing visions about marriage, and communicating physically—including sexually—two people are able to develop a special, meaningful, spiritual relationship. Out of the relationship comes love, the kind of love that children, friends, other relatives, and strangers can experience.

At times, due to lack of knowledge, life experiences, or a physical problem, intimacy is "short-circuited" physically. Sexual problems such as premature ejaculation, secondary impotence, or vaginismus can adversely affect the natural joy of physical communication and sexual intimacy.

Sex therapists are specially educated mental health professionals (psychologists, psychiatrists, etc.). These professionals can be found through a gynecologist, a psychologist, or a counseling center. When you go in for a treatment plan, the sex therapist will take your history. The approach will include hints on improving communication and understanding. The cure rate is one of the highest in the field of psychology. For some problems, the cure rate is over 99 percent.

One of the cornerstones of the approach is called "sensate focus," an exercise that improves physical sensitivity and encourages relaxation. This exercise and others used generally come from the work of Masters and Johnson and Helen Singer Kaplan. The medically sound, psychologically helpful, and religiously appropriate information has helped good marriages, suffering because of sexual difficulties, to become stronger.

Probably the biggest caution is that sex therapy should not be seen as a solution to a totally incompatible relationship or as a substitute

Self-Care for Every Day

for marriage counseling when there are a number of serious problems (including sexuality) in the relationship. However, sex therapy can help a Christian couple move through a physical block to intimacy so that their relationship becomes even more alive and vital and thus can strengthen family life.

References and Bibliography

Augsburger, David. *Anger and Assertiveness in Pastoral Care*. Philadelphia: Fortress Press, 1979.

Bloom, Anthony. *Beginning to Pray*. Mahwah, N.J.: Paulist Press, 1982.

Burns, David. *Feeling Good: The New Mood Therapy*. New York: New American Library, 1981.

Catoir, John. *Enjoy the Lord*. Waldwick, N.J.: Arena Lettres, 1979.

Cousins, Norman. *Anatomy of an Illness*. New York: Norton, 1980.

Delfieux, Pierre-Marie. *The Jerusalem Community Rule of Life*. Mahwah, N.J.: Paulist Press, 1985.

DeMello, Anthony. *One Minute Wisdom*. New York: Doubleday Publishing Co., 1986.

Faricy, Robert, S.J. and Wicks, Robert. *Contemplating Jesus*. Mahwah, N.J.: Paulist Press, 1986.

Fenhagen, J. *Invitation to Holiness*. San Francisco: Harper & Row Publishers, 1985.

Foster, Richard. *Celebration of Discipline: Paths to Spiritual Growth*. New York: Harper & Row Publishers, 1978.

Gonzales-Balado, Jose L., and Playfoot, Janet, eds. *My Life for the Poor: The Story of Mother Teresa in Her Own Words*. San Francisco: Harper & Row Publishers, 1985.

Hauser, Richard. *In His Spirit*. Mahwah, N.J.: Paulist Press, 1982.

Holmes, Urban, III. *Spirituality for Ministry*. New York: Harper & Row Publishers, 1982.

Johnston, William, S.J. *Christian Mysticism Today*. New York: Harper & Row Publishers, 1984.

Self-Care for Every Day

Kushner, Harold S. *When Bad Things Happen to Good People*. New York: Schocken Books, 1981.

Leech, Kenneth. *True Prayer: An Invitation to Christian Spirituality*. New York: Harper & Row Publishers, 1981.

Lewis, C.S. *Surprised by Joy*. New York: Harcourt, Brace & Co., 1955.

Merton, Thomas, O.C.S.O. *New Seeds of Contemplation*. New York: New Directions, 1961.

Navone, John, S.J. *A Theology of Failure*. Mahwah, N.J.: Paulist Press, 1974.

Nouwen, Henri. *Making All Things New: An Invitation to Life in the Spirit*. New York: Harper & Row Publishers, 1981.

Nouwen, Henri. *Reaching Out*. New York: Doubleday Publishing Co., 1975.

Nouwen, Henri. *The Living Reminder: Service and Prayer in Memory of Jesus Christ*. Minneapolis: Winston Press, 1981.

Nouwen, Henri. *Way of the Heart*. New York: Ballantine Books, 1983.

Palmer, Parker. "The Spiritual Life: Apocalypse Now." *Living with the Apocalypse*. Edited by Tilden Edwards. New York: Harper & Row Publishers, 1984.

Steindl-Rast, David. *Gratefulness, the Heart of Prayer: An Approach to Life in Fullness*. Mahwah, N.J.: Paulist Press, 1984.

Underwood, Ralph. *Empathy and Confrontation in Pastoral Care*. Philadelphia: Westminster, 1985.

Whitehead, James. "An Asceticism of Time." *Review for Religious*, Vol. 39, 1980.

Wicks, Robert J. *Availability...The Problem and the Gift*. Mahwah, N.J.: Paulist Press, 1986.

Wicks, Robert J. *Self-Ministry through Self-Understanding*. Chicago: Loyola University Press, 1990.

Wicks, Robert J. *Helping Others: Ways of Listening, Sharing, Counseling*. New York: Gardner Press, 1982.